D0428979

THE BELLES OF

BASEBALL

THE ALL-AMERICAN GIRLS
PROFESSIONAL BASEBALL LEAGUE

BY NEL YOMTOV

CONTENT CONSULTANT
KAT WILLIAMS, PHD
ASSOCIATE PROFESSOR OF AMERICAN HISTORY
MARSHALL UNIVERSITY

Essential Library

An Imprint of Abdo Publishing | abdopublishing.com

ABDOPUBLISHING.COM

Published by Abdo Publishing, a division of ABDO, PO Box 398166, Minneapolis, Minnesota 55439. Copyright © 2017 by Abdo Consulting Group, Inc. International copyrights reserved in all countries. No part of this book may be reproduced in any form without written permission from the publisher. Essential Library™ is a trademark and logo of Abdo Publishing.

Printed in the United States of America, North Mankato, Minnesota
102016
012017

THIS BOOK CONTAINS RECYCLED MATERIALS

Cover Photo: Bettman/Getty Images
Interior Photos: Courtesy of The History Museum, 4–5, 11, 36, 38, 56–57, 59, 70, 72, 74–75, 79, 86; AP Images, 9; Library of Congress, 14–15; Bettman/Getty Images, 17, 26–27, 43; Mark Rucker/Transcendental Graphics/Getty Images, 21, 66–67; Wallace Kirkland/The LIFE Picture Collection/Getty Images, 40–41; Red Line Editorial, 49, 51, 91; Transcendental Graphics/Getty Images, 54–55; Mark Cunningham/MLB Photos/Getty Images, 65, 93; Shutterstock Images, 81; NBHOF Library, 82–83; John Olson/Getty Images, 88–89; Milo Stewart, Jr./NBHOF Library, 95; Columbia Pictures/Photofest, 97

Editor: Susan Bradley
Series Designer: Maggie Villaume

PUBLISHER'S CATALOGING-IN-PUBLICATION DATA

Names: Yomtov, Nel, author.
Title: The belles of baseball: the All-American Girls Professional Baseball League
    / by Nel Yomtov.
Other titles: The All-American Girls Professional Baseball League
Description: Minneapolis, MN : Abdo Publishing, 2017. | Series: Hidden heroes |
    Includes bibliographical references and index.
Identifiers: LCCN 2016945478 | ISBN 9781680783865 (lib. bdg.) |
    ISBN 9781680797398 (ebook)
Subjects: LCSH: Baseball for women--Juvenile literature. | Women baseball
    players--Juvenile literature. | Baseball--Juvenile literature. | All-American
    Girls Professional Baseball League--Juvenile literature.
Classification: DDC 796.357--dc23
LC record available at http://lccn.loc.gov/2016945478

CONTENTS

CHAPTER ONE
PLAY BALL!

It was Sunday, September 17, 1950, at Beyer Stadium in Rockford, Illinois. The final game of the best-of-seven championship series between the Rockford Peaches and the Fort Wayne Daisies had been played earlier in the day. The Peaches crushed the powerful Daisies, 11–0, to win the All-American Girls Professional Baseball League (AAGPBL) title—the team's fourth championship in eight years.

The stars of the game were Rockford pitcher Nickie Fox and slugging first basewoman Dorothy Kamenshek. Fox, the owner of a 14–12 record during the regular season, racked up her third victory in the championship series, the only pitcher in the league to ever accomplish that feat.

Batter Dorothy Harrell was a star player in her eight seasons with the popular Rockford Peaches, one of the founding teams of the AAGPBL.

Kamenshek slammed four hits, including a home run and a triple, while scoring five runs and driving in two.

Rockford's assault began in the first inning against Fort Wayne's starting pitcher, Millie Deegan. Deegan, a crafty right-hander, hit two batters and walked a third to load the bases. Jackie Kelley then slashed a single to drive home two runs. In the second inning, with Marilyn Jones on first base with two outs, Deegan surrendered a long home run to Kamenshek. The score stood at 4–0.

Fort Wayne reliever Dottie Collins fared little better. In the third inning, Eleanor Callow greeted Collins with a ringing double and scored on a Charlene Barnett single. Rockford roughed up Collins for four more runs in the fourth inning. The big play was a double error by Fort Wayne infielder Evelyn Wawryshyn that allowed two runs to score. Rockford closed out the scoring with runs in the sixth and eighth innings to notch the 11–0 shutout.

This Game Seven showdown was a fitting climax to the hard-fought championship series. Playing in front of an enthusiastic home crowd, Rockford had won the first game, 3–1, paced by a 15-hit attack and the stellar pitching of Fox. The Peaches won Game Two, 7–2, scoring all its runs in a wild second inning. For Game Three, the series moved to Fort Wayne's Zollner Stadium, where the Daisies topped Rockford, 7–3, on a wet and rainy night. The Daisies evened the series in Game Four, 5–3, on a strong pitching performance by Maxine Kline, the winner of 23 regular-season games.

Game Five was a nail-biter, won by Rockford in ten innings, 4–3. The Peaches scored two runs in the top of the tenth inning on an infield hit and a steal of home plate to pull ahead, 4–2. Fort Wayne threatened to tie the score in the bottom half of the inning but fell short by one run. With its victory, the Peaches held the series lead, three games to two. The series shifted back to Rockford, where the Daisies rapped out an easy 8–0 victory to set up the dramatic Game Seven finale.

Baseball has traditionally been considered a man's sport. Even in modern times, newspaper and magazine articles, online features,

SECRET ORIGINS?

Despite baseball being one of the world's most popular games, the exact origins of the sport are unknown. Many historians agree baseball evolved from a combination of English folk games, including stoolball, cricket, and rounders. Stoolball involved a pitcher tossing a ball toward either a milking stool or a piece of wood mounted on a stake known as a wicket. A batter defended the wicket by hitting the ball and running between wickets to score a run. In rounders, players hit a leather-cased ball with a bat and scored by running around four bases on the field. Various versions of a bat-and-ball game were played in rural parts of America as early as the 1740s. By the early 1800s, the game had spread to larger cities.

and television programming generally depict women as spectators—not as active participants in the sport. Though it's not widely known, women have been playing organized baseball in the United States for approximately 150 years. They currently play recreational, amateur, and semipro games on Little League teams, on college squads, and in international tournaments. And the women of the AAGPBL played high-quality, competitive baseball more than 70 years ago.

Hidden Heroines

In 1943, Philip K. Wrigley, the owner of Major League Baseball's Chicago Cubs and president of the Wrigley Chewing Gum Company, formed what came to be known as the All-American Girls Professional Baseball League. His goal was to provide inexpensive entertainment to residents of midwestern towns and cities after the United States' 1941 entry into World War II (1939–1945). He also sought to encourage the public's continued interest in baseball so fans would still support it after the war. Many of the townspeople supported the war effort by working in nearby factories that produced planes, vehicles, and other essential materials.

During its 12 seasons, from 1943 to 1954, the league recruited more than 550 women ballplayers. They came from all parts of the United States, Canada, and even

Philip Wrigley, owner of the Chicago Cubs, founded the AAGPBL to
keep fans interested in baseball during World War II.

Cuba. Most of the women were in their late teens or early 20s. Several players were only 15 years old when they were signed by the league to play. The women came mainly from working-class families, and many had grown up on farms.

These young athletes were drawn to the league for one reason: they loved to play baseball. According to former AAGPBL player Lois J. Youngen:

They loved to win, they loved to make a great catch, they loved to feel the crack of the wooden bat on the ball and to know it would be a base hit. . . . Playing baseball was more important than the money (as long as you had enough to survive).[1]

Young women from many states and Canada tried out for the AAGPBL to pursue their dreams of playing baseball.

The women who joined the AAGPBL were outstanding, accomplished athletes. Pitcher Jean Faut played eight years in the league, posting a lifetime win-loss record of 140–64, with a 1.23 earned run average (ERA). Doris Sams served double duty as an outfielder and a pitcher. She notched a lifetime batting average of .290 and was twice named the AAGPBL's Player of the Year. Strikeout queen Collins won 20 or more games in four consecutive seasons and won 117 games in her six-year career. The best all-around player in the league, Kamenshek, was a hard-hitting first basewoman who won two batting titles and finished her career with a .293 batting average, among the highest in league history.

Through the years, the AAGPBL underwent numerous changes in rules, ball size, and field layout. Originally established as a softball league with standard underhand pitching, the league continually evolved toward regulation men's baseball. Distances to the pitcher's mound and between the bases were lengthened. An increasingly smaller ball was used. Base stealing and leading off the bases were permitted. Through it all, highly skilled women athletes successfully adapted to a rough-and-tumble version of male baseball.

For much of its existence, the AAGPBL was a resounding success. In one year alone, nearly one million fans poured into ballparks to watch the women perform. In time, according to author Barbara Gregorich, even "the men who managed them came to believe there was nothing these women couldn't do."[5]

Playing professional baseball wasn't an easy life, and the women of the AAGPBL endured many hardships and inconveniences. But nothing could prevent them from playing baseball.

Baseball's Female Barrier Breakers

The women of the AAGPBL were up to the challenge of playing exciting, action-packed hardball—and more. By skillfully playing what was generally considered a male sport with power, speed, and grace, they challenged society's notions of women's roles in the World War II era. The players also provided a critical morale boost to a nation enduring a bloody and costly war. Their endeavor was truly patriotic.

The AAGPBL provided women the opportunity to play in front of packed stadiums of loyal and adoring fans. By living their dreams, these unheralded women helped pave the way for millions of other female athletes in the years that followed.

CHAPTER TWO
NOT FOR BOYS ONLY

By the 1830s, baseball was already widely played in the United States. In 1845, the New York Knickerbocker Club, one of the earliest teams to play a formal game of baseball, established a set of playing rules. By the late 1860s, men's professional baseball teams were formed throughout the eastern United States to play in front of paying customers. Young Americans passionately embraced the sport, and the game's popularity soared.

The rules of early baseball differed greatly from the modern game's rules. Among the numerous distinctions were a lighter and smaller ball, the use of underhand pitching delivery, and a shorter distance between the

Men's professional baseball began in the late 1860s. Within several decades, there were dozens of professional leagues throughout the eastern United States.

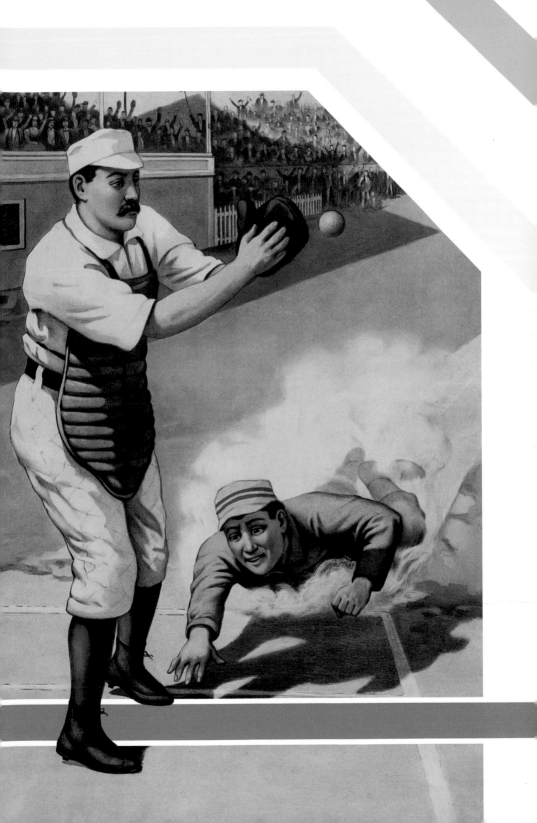

pitcher and home plate. By the 1890s, however, the game more closely resembled today's baseball.

An Unladylike Sport?

The meteoric rise of baseball occurred during the Victorian era, from approximately 1876 to 1900. During this period, women were viewed as the weaker and gentler sex. A woman's role was to have children and take care of the home and her husband. Physical activity was off limits; sports and strenuous activities were for men only. These activities were considered unladylike, and only a coarse, unsophisticated woman would engage in such behavior. Doctors and medical authorities even claimed physical exertion could harm women, resulting in nervous conditions and impaired offspring.

But by this time, America was in love with baseball. The game had captured the national values of adventure, competition, and sportsmanship. Baseball had become the nation's sport and the national pastime. Despite the warnings and restrictive codes of behavior for women, many women were eager and determined to play baseball.

Joining the Game

Women's colleges, particularly in the eastern United States, provided the first opportunity for women to participate in organized baseball. At these institutions,

The earliest women's baseball teams were formed at women's colleges, where students were urged to be physically active as part of their education.

women were encouraged to reach their fullest potential, both intellectually and physically. In addition to taking courses in science, mathematics, history, and other disciplines, students were urged to engage in outdoor activities such as ice-skating. Baseball instruction was often offered as part of the colleges' physical education programs. According to author Gai Ingham Berlage:

> The "new woman," the educated, independent, athletic type who was a product of these schools, represented a radical departure from the "true woman," the weak, passive, frail, dependent woman of the Victorian ideal.[1]

Vassar College had the earliest women's baseball teams, in 1866. The teams played with eight rather than the standard nine players. Other women's colleges soon fielded teams: Smith in 1879, Mount Holyoke in 1891, and Wellesley in 1897. Most of the early games were played between teams from the same college. This is called intramural baseball, involving different classes, dormitories, or baseball clubs. The players' uniforms often consisted of a long dress with long sleeves. It was common for players to catch or stop balls with their skirt. Teams typically used standard baseball equipment, including a hardball and baseball gloves.

In the early days of women's collegiate baseball, schools played various modified versions of the game. Rules permitted different-sized diamonds and balls and allowed either underhand or overhand pitching. Few women's colleges played by official men's rules.

In time, women outside of the colleges began taking up baseball. The number of women playing the game slowly but steadily increased. In 1867, an all-African-American women's team called the Dolly Vardens formed in Philadelphia, Pennsylvania, becoming the first professional baseball club for either men or women. The players competed while wearing corsets,

> "Please ask Morgan [older brother] if he has a baseball mitt he can send me. We are practicing all the time now, and trying curves, and playing with a real baseball."[2]
>
> —Margaret Townsend, Class of 1911, Smith College, in a letter written to her parents, April 20, 1908

long skirts, and high-button shoes. Almost immediately, male promoters attempted to cash in on the potential appeal of women's baseball. In 1875, three promoters formed two women's teams, the Blondes and the Brunettes, as a publicity gimmick. The teams played their first game of modified baseball on September 11 in Springfield, Illinois. Bases were 50 feet (15 m) apart instead of 90 feet (27 m), and a lighter ball was used.

News accounts suggest the players were selected more for their beauty than their ball-playing abilities. One reporter wrote, "The attraction is the novelty of seeing eighteen girls prettily attired in gymnastic dress playing in a game of baseball."[3]

The Young Ladies Baseball Clubs

Two further attempts to establish organized women's baseball teams were made in the late 1800s. In August 1883, the Young Ladies Baseball Club was formed.

THE
BLOOMER GIRLS

Beginning in the 1890s, teams of skilled women baseball players organized to play baseball professionally. Called Bloomer Girls after an early style of pants worn by women, the teams were composed of both women and men. The teams barnstormed, or traveled, throughout the northeastern and midwestern United States, as well as Canada, playing against all-men's amateur and semipro teams. Initially, the men dressed as women, donning curly wigs and skirts. By the early 1900s, women abandoned their bloomers and skirts and wore standard baseball pants.

Reactions to the Bloomer Girls ranged from praise to angry outrage. A sports reporter covering a Bloomer Girls team for the *Cincinnati Enquirer* wrote, "The girls played as if their lives depended on winning the game . . . (they) kept working hard for victory."[4] Many writers, however, believed the women lacked the necessary skills to play baseball at a high level. "The women cannot play baseball and never will be able to learn how to play the game," declared one writer in the *New York Tribune*.[5] In fact, much of the public viewed the women playing a "men's" game as unfeminine and tough.

Despite the criticism, hundreds of Bloomer Girls teams sprouted up throughout the country, including Texas, Illinois, New York, Massachusetts, and Missouri. Many squads produced outstanding women ballplayers, such as Lizzie Arlington and Lizzie Murphy. One team that formed near the end of the Bloomer Girl era, the

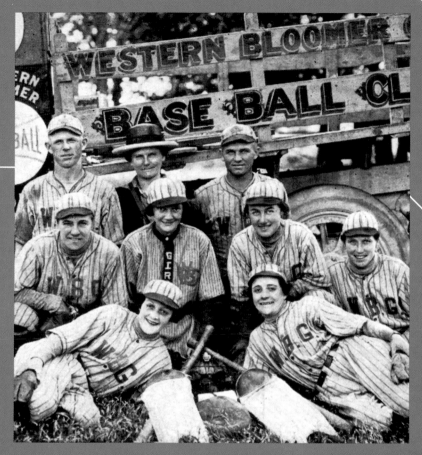

From the 1890s to the 1930s, men and women played together on Bloomer Girls teams, competing against all-male teams in the towns they visited.

Philadelphia Bobbies, traveled to Japan in 1925 to play exhibition games against men's teams. The shortstop for the Bobbies, Edith Houghton, was only 13 years old at the time, having joined the team at age ten. By the 1930s, Bloomer Girls teams dwindled, due in large part to the growing popularity of organized women's softball leagues throughout the United States.

With an emphasis on novelty and entertainment rather than playing skills, the Philadelphia club played its first game on August 18 to a crowd of 500 amused spectators.[6] The Young Ladies squad folded after two years, but not before appearing in several large cities such as Chicago, Illinois, and New Orleans, Louisiana. In an 1884 trip through the southern United States, a group of the players competed against local men's teams.

In 1890, promoter W. S. Franklin organized the Young Ladies Baseball Club #1 to play against men's teams across the United States and Canada. The players on the team ranged in age from 17 to 22. On the field, they wore dresses, scarves, dark stockings, and ankle-high leather shoes. Despite their bulky uniforms, the women "still managed to annihilate the men's teams they played."[7] The women baseball pioneers of the Young Ladies Baseball Clubs demonstrated how serious they were about playing the game they loved.

The Barriers Begin to Come Down

Despite the general public's view of women in baseball as a curiosity, several women cracked open the door to professional baseball. One of these pioneers was Lizzie Arlington. Arlington learned to play baseball with her father and brothers in their Pennsylvania coal-mining town. Having impressed league president Ed Barrow with her pitching skills, on July 5, 1898, Arlington became the first woman to appear in a men's professional baseball game. The novelty of a woman ballplayer failed to attract large crowds, however, and Arlington's contract was soon terminated.

In 1918, Lizzie Murphy of Rhode Island, known as "Spike," signed on with a men's semipro team at age 15. In 1922, she played in an exhibition game with American League and New England all-stars against the Boston Red Sox. It was the first time a woman played in a game with a major league baseball club. Murphy, known to fans as the "Queen of Baseball," retired from the game at age 41.

JACKIE MITCHELL: STRIKEOUT ACE

In early 1931, Joe Engel, owner of the minor league Chattanooga (Tennessee) Lookouts, was seeking to boost attendance for his team's upcoming season. As a publicity gimmick, Engel signed 17-year-old left-handed pitcher Jackie Mitchell, a local female baseball star, to help attract the fans. Engel then announced Mitchell would pitch in an exhibition game against the New York Yankees. The news made national headlines, and on April 2, 1931, approximately 4,000 fans poured into the Chattanooga ballpark to witness the historic event. The third batter Mitchell faced was the great Babe Ruth, whom she struck out on four pitches. Lou Gehrig then strode to the batter's box. Mitchell fired three pitches, and Gehrig swung and missed each one. The fans roared with delight. In mere moments, the teenage sensation had struck out two of the greatest players in baseball history.

In 1931, Jackie Mitchell, a 17-year-old pitching sensation, was signed to a minor-league contract with the Chattanooga Lookouts. Her contract was voided a few days later by Commissioner Kenesaw Mountain Landis, who deemed baseball too strenuous for a woman. Despite the impact of Arlington, Murphy, Mitchell, and a few others, women were largely excluded from professional baseball well into the twentieth century.

Women and Softball

Wrigley's AAGPBL was initially established as a softball league. The players in the league came from women's softball squads throughout the United States and Canada. First played in Chicago in November 1887, softball had become enormously popular. Everyone—men, women, and youngsters—played softball, a modified form of regulation baseball. They played on sandlots, on playgrounds, in gymnasiums, on beaches, and in parks.

Softball became popular, in part, because of a few key differences with baseball. The base paths were shorter, making them easier to run, as was the distance between the pitcher and the hitter. The larger ball was easier to hit. Games lasted only seven innings, rather than baseball's nine innings. The underhand pitching delivery was a smoother, less demanding motion than overhand pitching.

The sport's unisex appeal made softball, not baseball, the national pastime. By the mid-1930s, the United States boasted more than two million players on 60,000 organized teams. By 1942, nearly 200,000 men's and women's softball teams existed in the country. Civic groups, banks, restaurants, and local businesses of all types sponsored many of the women's teams.

Wrigley was well aware of softball's popularity. In his home city of Chicago alone, one women's league of only four teams attracted more than 250,000 fans in the 1942 season. Wrigley also supported women's participation in sports—as either active participants or spectators. Each year, he allowed a ballpark he owned in Los Angeles, California, to be used for the women's and men's state softball championships. In Chicago, Wrigley established a weekly Ladies Day at Wrigley Field, home of the Chicago Cubs. Tens of thousands of women poured through the turnstiles each year, thoroughly convincing him that women and baseball were a perfect—and marketable—fit. Wrigley didn't wait long to take action.

"It has been no secret to sports fans in the Midwest that girls' softball in Chicago has been outdrawing the major-league baseball clubs."[8]

—Herb Graffis in "Belles of the Ballgame," Liberty magazine, October 16, 1943

CHAPTER THREE

THE BIRTH OF THE AAGPBL

On Sunday, December 7, 1941, Japanese aircraft attacked the US naval fleet stationed at Pearl Harbor in Hawaii. The United States declared war, drawn into an overseas conflict that had been raging for more than two years. Immediately, tens of thousands of American men joined the armed forces and were sent to distant battlefields throughout Europe, Africa, Asia, and the Pacific. In all, more than 16 million Americans served their nation's military during the war, including nearly 350,000 women who wore the uniform either at home or abroad.[1]

Average Americans also contributed to the war effort at home. Gasoline, meat, metal,

Major league slugger Ted Williams, *left*, set aside his career as an all-star to enlist in the US Navy in 1942.

rubber, and many other foods and items were rationed so there would be enough for the troops. Nonmilitary train travel was restricted to conserve fuel and provide preferential travel arrangements to military personnel.

Perhaps the most significant change on the home front was the role of women in American society. In the years following World War I (1914–1918), women were urged to be housekeepers and raise children, after having worked in factories during the war. Now, they were again being asked to replace men in factories. There, the women worked to produce the planes, ships, weapons, and other supplies needed to fight the war. Between April 1940 and August 1943, approximately three million women entered the labor force.[2] They worked not only in the factories that produced military equipment, but also in the world of sport as umpires, coaches, golf caddies, and even jockeys.

In this atmosphere of sacrifice, uncertainty, and social change, baseball found itself in a difficult position. How would it respond to the challenges of the war?

Baseball and World War II

Similar to most other able-bodied American males, dozens of professional baseball players were drafted or volunteered to serve in the armed forces. Many of the game's top stars, such as major leaguers Ted Williams, Stan Musial, and Hank Greenberg, hung up their cleats and joined the war effort. So many players served in the military during the war that the roster of every major league team was severely depleted. The number of players in the minor leagues dwindled as well, causing many leagues to shut down. Ballplayers who did not serve in the military often put aside their baseball careers to work in war industries. Philip Wrigley even scrapped plans to install lights at Wrigley Field in 1942, donating them to the US Navy instead. With fewer stars to watch and travel restrictions in place, attendance at major and minor league games dropped sharply.

Worried about the war's effect on the sport, Major League Baseball Commissioner Landis considered suspending baseball operations for the duration of the war.

PHILIP K. WRIGLEY: PATRIOTIC BUSINESSMAN

In 1943, 49-year-old Wrigley was president of the Wrigley Chewing Gum Company and owner of the Chicago Cubs. In addition to being a wealthy man, Wrigley was highly patriotic. In March 1941, nine months before Japan bombed Pearl Harbor, Wrigley sent his entire inventory of 500,000 pounds (227,000 kg) of aluminum, used in gum wrappers, to the US government. He later loaned the government South Catalina Island, property he owned off the coast of Southern California, for military training. Wrigley also had his workers who tapped gum trees in Central and South America tap rubber trees to provide a much-needed resource for the US war effort. Wrigley died in 1977 at age 83.

In January 1942, he wrote a letter to President Franklin D. Roosevelt to express his concerns. Days later, the president responded: "I honestly feel it would be best for the country to keep baseball going . . . these players are a definite recreational asset . . . to their fellow citizens—and that in my judgment is thoroughly worthwhile."[3]

Wrigley kept a sharp eye on these developments. Like Landis, he was concerned about the future of baseball during the war, which he believed would not end soon. If baseball was to have a long-term future, it *must* survive during the war, he concluded. But how?

Wrigley's solution was startling—and radical. Professional teams of women athletes, he decided, would be the nation's wartime ballplayers.

The Plan Unfolds

As early as the winter of 1942, Wrigley assembled a team of assistants to study the feasibility of a professional women's league. His team included advertising executive Arthur Meyerhoff, lawyer Paul Harper, and Ann Harnett, who had organized women's softball teams in Chicago. Wrigley was keenly aware of the immense popularity of women's softball throughout the United States and the potential of women as baseball fans. He was convinced his plan was sound. In January 1943, the committee returned with encouraging news about the appeal of a professional women's softball league.

The next month, Wrigley presented his idea to the owners of the other seven teams in the National League. He hoped they would allow his women ballplayers to use their stadiums when their major league men's team was out of town. The owners turned him down. They believed Wrigley's idea could not succeed.

Wrigley refused to let his idea die. If he couldn't use the other National League stadiums (located in New York, New York; Saint Louis, Missouri; Cincinnati, Ohio; Boston, Massachusetts; and Pittsburgh and Philadelphia, Pennsylvania), he would organize teams in the Midwest, closer to his hometown of Chicago. The teams' home cities would be close to one another to conform to wartime gas rationing and travel restrictions.

The next step was to establish the teams in the new league. Wrigley decided a city could obtain a franchise for a fee of $22,500. Wrigley would match that amount with his own funds. The league would handle publicity and provide uniforms and equipment. It would also recruit and train the players and assign them to each

> "The League will be good for your community, good for the country, good for the war effort, and good for you."[4]
>
> —Philip Wrigley to potential league franchisees

team to ensure balanced competition. The league, not the teams, would pay the players' salaries. Each team would have 15 players. In later years, team rosters would be increased to 18 players.

Wrigley named his new organization the All-American Girls Softball League. It was to be a hybrid form of softball and baseball. The underhand softball pitching delivery would be used, but the base paths and pitching distances would be lengthened. The games would last nine innings instead of softball's seven, and runners would be permitted to lead off base and steal. The ball would be slightly smaller than a softball.

Four cities raised money for a franchise. They were Rockford (the Peaches); South Bend, Indiana (the Blue Sox); and Racine and Kenosha, Wisconsin (the Belles and the Comets). Each city was home to war industries or located near communities that produced goods used in the war. Wrigley's new enterprise would help serve a patriotic purpose: offering entertainment to the men and women working in America's war factories. Now it was time for Wrigley to find his women ballplayers.

The Call Goes Out

Fueled by newspaper reports, word about Wrigley's new women's softball league spread quickly throughout the Midwest and Canada. Wrigley sent out his Chicago Cubs' talent scouts to search for the best women players. The scouts focused on finding players near the four host cities.

Hundreds of women turned up for the first tryouts, conducted in 12 large cities. By May 1943, approximately 280 women had made the first cut and were invited to Wrigley Field in Chicago for the final tryouts and selection. The recruits hailed from 26 states and five Canadian provinces. The league paid for the women's transportation to Chicago.

Some of the recruits were as young as 15, with many only 17 or 18. For some, especially those from farms or rural areas, it was their first time visiting a big

GENERAL RULES OF THE AAGPBL

The official rules given to each player in the AAGPBL read in part as follows:

1. *ALWAYS appear in feminine attire when not actively engaged in practice or playing ball.*

2. *Smoking or drinking is not permissible in public places. Liquor drinking will not be permissible under any circumstances.*

3. *All social engagements must be approved by chaperone.*

4. *All living quarters and eating places must be approved by the chaperones.*

5. *Due to shortage of equipment, baseballs must not be given as souvenirs without permission from the management.*

6. *In order to sustain the complete spirit of rivalry between clubs, the members of the different clubs must not fraternize at any time during the season. Friendly discussions in lobbies with opposing players are permissible.*[5]

city—for others, the first time leaving their hometowns. Imagine the excitement and anticipation the young women experienced on their train rides to Chicago. Some of the women had never even ridden on a train.

Above all, however, the women had the opportunity to play baseball—the game they loved. "It was a chance to get paid for something I would have done for free," said catcher Tuffy Hickson.[6] But those who made the final cut didn't have to work for free. The players' salaries, ranging from $45 to $85 weekly plus expenses, were more than what the average wage earner made at the time, approximately $40 per week.[7]

Selling Femininity

Wrigley realized the success of his All-American Girls Softball League depended on the support of the public. He wanted his league to be seen as wholesome, family-friendly entertainment. His women players would not mirror the rough-and-tumble image of Bloomer Girls. Nor would they be characterized by the popular notion that women's softball was too masculine. Instead, Wrigley stressed the femininity of his players. Recruits were selected almost as much for their physical appearance and character as they were for their playing ability.

Official league documents demonstrate Wrigley's desire to play up the femininity angle. A letter to potential players in 1943 read, "The All-American Girls Softball League is created with the highest ideals of womanhood in mind. . . . The natural appeal of women in every walk of life will be brought out in this venture. Girls will dress, act, and carry themselves as befits the feminine sex."[8]

To achieve his goal, Wrigley and his staff designed a girlish player's uniform, hired team chaperones to monitor the activities of the players, and established strict codes of conduct. In the teams' home cities, the players would live with local families to further enhance the clean-cut image Wrigley wished to portray.

But Wrigley didn't stop there. Acting on the advice of his advertising consultant, Meyerhoff, the league established a charm school to teach the

AN IMPRACTICAL UNIFORM

To increase fan appeal, the league uniform aimed for a feminine and attractive look, but its design was totally impractical for playing baseball. The official uniform consisted of a short-sleeved, one-piece dress. The flared skirt could be worn no shorter than six inches (15 cm) above the knee. Knee-high socks and a small cap with a large peak completed the uniform. Underneath, the players wore satin boxer shorts. Players suffered painful thigh bruises called strawberries from sliding with bare legs. Pitchers also discovered the flared skirt interfered with their underhand pitching delivery. "It was great from the spectator viewpoint," said Racine Belles pitcher Joanne Winter. "From our standpoint, not many of us enjoyed it. If I'd had a brain and a seamstress, I would have changed it."[9]

A chaperone, *right*, provided peace of mind for parents of younger players who played in cities far from home.

> "She took care of all our problems: our jewelry, our money, our chewing gum, our sewing, our [personal] problems, our strawberries [sliding bruises], and our dislocated fingers. . . . She had spunk, spark, and fight, and we all respected her."[10]
>
> —Marilyn Jenkins, former Grand Rapids Chicks catcher, about chaperone Dorothy Hunter

young women the finer points of manners and personal grooming. At spring training in 1943, for example, after hours of practicing on the field, the women attended classes run by the Helena Rubenstein Salon. They took lessons in applying makeup, choosing clothes, and even in walking, speaking properly, and sitting upright in a feminine style.

Press releases highlighted not only the women's ball-playing skills but their physical attributes as well. Catcher Helen Westerman was described as a "petite, blue-eyed blonde weighing only 95 pounds (43 kg), fragilely built."[11] Another catcher, Bonnie Baker, was reported to have a "gorgeous smile, dark eyes fringed by long lashes. . . . [She has] a truly regal bearing and knows how to wear clothes to set off her tall beauty."[12]

1943: The First Year

The league's inaugural season began in mid-May 1943. Each of the four teams would play

Maintaining a feminine appearance and projecting a wholesome image were essential parts of life in the AAGPBL.

54 games, totaling 108 games for the whole league. The players' schedule was grueling and nonstop. During the summer months, June through August, the women played seven days a week, with doubleheaders on Sunday. Players were often traded in midseason to balance the talent on each squad. The Racine Belles won the league championship, beating the Kenosha Comets in the Francis J. Shaughnessy Playoffs.

The season was highlighted by many promotional efforts. Patriotic, war-related publicity events, such as special nights for specific war industries and free admission for military personnel, were common. Several exhibition games were played at nearby military bases and veterans' hospitals. An all-star game was played at Wrigley Field on the evening of July 1—the first night game ever played at the stadium. The free event was part of a Women's Army Air Corps recruiting rally, complete with a marching band, military drills, and recruiting speeches.

Initial reaction to the league—and Wrigley's so-called belles of baseball—was positive but not overwhelming. To improve the game's appeal by distinguishing it from softball and making its rules more baseball-like, Wrigley changed the league name to the All-American Girls Baseball League during the 1943 season and then again to the All-American Girls Professional Ball League. Rule changes introduced in subsequent years made the game more closely resemble men's regulation baseball.

By season's end, Wrigley was optimistic about his venture. More than 176,000 fans attended games, and the press and baseball fans appreciated the quality of the women's play.[14] The four host cities enthusiastically supported their teams. Wrigley began planning his next move: expansion.

CHAPTER FOUR

THE RISE AND DECLINE OF THE AAGPBL

In its first year, the AAGPBL was a moderate success—yet it hadn't earned a single penny in profit. In fact, Wrigley never planned for the league to make money. Under his leadership, the AAGPBL was formed as a nonprofit organization. Any profit was used to support local projects. Now, at the end of the first season, the AAGPBL mastermind looked to build upon the first-year accomplishments of his groundbreaking operation.

1944

By early 1944, Wrigley decided to add two new cities to the league: Milwaukee,

All the league's teams gathered for spring training each year. Locations included Illinois, Mississippi, Florida, and Cuba.

Wisconsin, and Minneapolis, Minnesota. Both teams, however, were short-lived. The Minneapolis Millerettes were based approximately 400 miles (640 km) from their nearest competitor in Rockford. Opposing teams arrived in Minneapolis exhausted from the grueling trip. Within weeks, the league folded the team, but kept it playing nonleague, road-only games as the Orphans. In 1945, Fort Wayne, Indiana, adopted the Millerettes and renamed them the Daisies. The Milwaukee Chicks folded at the end of the 1944 season due largely to poor attendance and weak local support.

Both Milwaukee and Minneapolis were large cities. Each offered many other sports options, including men's minor league baseball. In the end, sports fans in those cities preferred to pay to see men's teams play ball.

The AAGPBL instituted a few subtle changes in field layout and ball size. It mattered little to the women, however, who were quickly developing friendships and playing a game they enjoyed.

When the 1944 season ended, Kenosha and Milwaukee faced off in the play-offs. Amazingly, Milwaukee, which had endured such poor fan support, won the championship. League attendance for the year rose to more than 260,000.[1] Talented players, such as second basewoman Sophie Kurys and pitchers Collins and Connie

Sophie Kurys of the Racine Belles, known as "the Flint
Flash," led the league in stolen bases. In 1946 alone, she stole
201 bases in 203 attempts.

Wisniewski, emerged as genuine stars, with many others
on the horizon.

After the play-offs, Wrigley wanted to devote more
time to overseeing his Chicago Cubs. He sold the league
to Meyerhoff's management corporation for $10,000. The
league continued to handle its previous responsibilities—
recruiting players, hiring managers, running spring
training, and handling publicity—but now on a for-profit
basis. The teams remained nonprofit—a circumstance
that would later cause friction between the corporation
and the individual team directors.

1945

The 1945 season opened with six teams—the initial four clubs plus two new squads, the Grand Rapids Chicks (formerly Milwaukee) and the Fort Wayne Daisies (the Millerette "Orphans").

As the gameplay moved closer to baseball, finding qualified players became increasingly difficult. Softball players often found the adjustment hard to make. In response, Meyerhoff and league president Max Carey hired more scouts, but even this move failed to discover much new talent. The shortage of talent would plague the league throughout its existence.

The third season was yet another successful campaign. Attendance boomed to 450,000, and by season's end, league officials were looking to expand to eight teams the following year.[2] On the field, Rockford Peaches first basewoman Kamenshek began her rise to stardom, leading the league in runs scored (80), while batting .274.

1946

The war was over, and returning military personnel were being reunited with their families. Prospects for the AAGPBL were high, as two new teams—the Muskegon (Michigan) Lassies and Peoria (Illinois) Redwings—joined the league, now with eight squads.

Spring training was conducted not in the cold climate of the Midwest as in previous years, but on the ball fields of Pascagoula, Mississippi. Players appreciated the move to warmer climes, but the housing conditions were awful. The barracks teemed with roaches and other insects. "The cockroaches were so big, they didn't scurry; they strolled," remarked South Bend outfielder Daisy Junor. "You could put saddles on 'em," added Wisniewski.[3]

The major change to the game was the introduction of a modified sidearm delivery. Pitchers could now use a curveball or a sinker. The sidearm motion also allowed for a harder, faster delivery. At first, for example, South Bend pitcher

WOMEN
TEAM MANAGERS

Six of the 40 team managers in the league's history were women. Each was used only to fill short-term needs, usually hired in the middle or at the end of a season. All of the women who served as managers had at least four years of playing time in the AAGPBL. The most notable woman manager was Bonnie Baker. In 1950, Kalamazoo Lassies' manager Lenny Zintak was replaced by Baker, an all-star catcher with the South Bend Blue Sox. Under Baker's guidance, the Lassies climbed out of the cellar in the ten-team league and finished in fourth place. Many of the male managers were former big-name ballplayers, such as Hall of Famers Jimmy Foxx, Dave Bancroft, and Max Carey. After managing the Milwaukee Chicks in 1944, Carey served as AAGPBL president until 1950, when he returned to managing.

Jean Faut didn't care for the sidearm, but as the season progressed, she mastered the motion, launching her as one of the league's best hurlers. To facilitate the switch to sidearm, the size of the ball was reduced from a circumference of 11.5 inches (29 cm) to 11 inches (28 cm).

The league set a new attendance record of more than 750,000 paying customers.[4] Baseball was alive and well in the eight midwestern cities of the AAGPBL.

1947

The new season started with Meyerhoff orchestrating the league's most exotic publicity move to date. In April, he sent more than 200 players and league officials to Havana, Cuba, for spring training. Tens of thousands of Cuban baseball fans poured into the Gran Stadium de Havana to watch the AAGPBL women play exhibition games. For many of the women players, the trip to Cuba was an unforgettable, once-in-a-lifetime opportunity. There the women came face-to-face with a different culture. They met new people and made new friends.

In the ongoing move toward baseball's overhand pitching, full sidearm delivery was required in the 1947 season. Pitching began to dominate the league as never before, as batters found it difficult to adapt to the new style. Underhand pitching ace Wisniewski converted to the new style but was unable to maintain her mastery on the mound. Winning 32 games in 1945 and 33 games in 1946, Wisniewski dropped to only 16 wins in 1947. "I simply couldn't do it," she said. "It hurt my arm every time."[7]

1948

The big news in the 1948 season was the adoption of overhand pitching and the expansion to ten teams. The addition of the Springfield (Illinois) Sallies and the Chicago Colleens led officials to create Eastern and Western divisions. The new squads, however, had weak rosters and were doomed to fail from their inception. Both teams became rookie touring teams after the 1948 season, traveling to nearly 50 cities in the eastern United States to promote the league and attract recruits.

In 1944, Wrigley had covered the costs out of his own pocket when Milwaukee and Minneapolis folded. Now, under Meyerhoff's management company, the teams were collectively responsible for the financial losses caused by the failed expansion cities. Many team directors were opposed to expansion, an idea Meyerhoff strongly supported.

The loss of the Chicago team indicated to league officials that women's baseball could not survive in cities where there were men's major league teams. Meyerhoff and others wondered if the league could survive at all playing only in small midwestern cities. Despite these difficulties, the league's attendance reached 910,000 in 1948, the most the AAGPBL would ever draw.[8]

The overhand delivery itself caused the league further concerns. Many underhand softball pitchers were unable to learn the delivery and the control necessary to pitch overhand. The motion is also harder on the arm, shoulder, and wrist, so it requires more rest between starts than the underhand softball delivery. The league found itself short of qualified pitchers.

1949 to 1954: The End of an Era

The failure of the Springfield Sallies and the Chicago Colleens cost the league thousands of dollars. In 1949, the other clubs, who were responsible for absorbing league financial losses, responded by reducing the league's budget for publicity and scouting. It was a shortsighted decision, as the budget cut meant the league was unable to adequately advertise itself, and it could not properly recruit new players.

Only two teams made a profit in 1949, and one broke even. The other five clubs had significant financial losses ranging between $15,000 and $27,000.[9] Attendance dropped to 585,000, the lowest since 1946.[10]

A total of 14 cities hosted an AAGPBL team during its 12 seasons of play. The teams in smaller cities were most successful in garnering fan support.

The league experienced more money woes in 1950. The nearly bankrupt Rockford Peaches and Peoria Redwings had to sell ownership shares to survive the season. The Grand Rapids Chicks completed the season only because the players and managers said they would play even if not paid. The Muskegon Lassies folded in midseason and relocated to Kalamazoo, Michigan. Overall league attendance fell to 482,000.[11]

To stem the growing financial losses, the league eliminated meal money for the players on the road. The decision upset many of the women, especially the veterans. The league had already lost approximately 25 veterans in 1949 and 1950. The money-saving decision served only to frustrate these experienced, quality players.

But on the field, the women continued to furnish fans with an action-packed brand of baseball. A new, livelier ball was introduced, which helped increase batting averages and make the game more exciting.

At the end of the 1950 season, the teams voted to buy out Meyerhoff's management corporation, which they blamed for their financial problems. Each team operated independently and was responsible for its own scouting, recruitment, and spring training.

Despite the changeover, attendance continued declining, resulting in lower revenues for the teams.

AAGPBL TEAMS, 1943–1954[12]

TEAM	YEARS
Kenosha (Wisconsin) Comets	1943–1951
Racine (Wisconsin) Belles	1943–1950*
Rockford (Illinois) Peaches	1943–1954
South Bend (Indiana) Blue Sox	1943–1954
Milwaukee (Wisconsin) Chicks	1944**
Minneapolis (Minnesota) Millerettes	1944***
Fort Wayne (Indiana) Daisies	1945–1954
Grand Rapids (Michigan) Chicks	1945–1954
Muskegon (Michigan) Lassies	1946–1950†
Peoria (Illinois) Redwings	1946–1951
Chicago (Illinois) Colleens	1948††
Springfield (Illinois) Sallies	1948††
Kalamazoo (Michigan) Lassies	1950–1954
Battle Creek (Michigan) Belles	1951–1952†††
Muskegon (Michigan) Belles	1953

* Moved to Battle Creek, Michigan, 1951   † Moved to Kalamazoo, 1950
** Moved to Grand Rapids, 1945   †† Touring team only
*** Became the Fort Wayne Daisies, 1945   ††† Moved to Muskegon, 1953

Fan interest was dwindling, perhaps due to the immense popularity of a new form of entertainment: television.

Media coverage decreased as well, reflecting the public's growing indifference to women's professional baseball.

The teams' individual financial losses continued to mount. In 1951, the AAGPBL fielded eight teams. Kenosha and Peoria folded before the start of the 1952 season, leaving only six teams to play the 1952 and 1953 seasons. By the end of 1953, total team debt was a hefty $80,000, prompting the league to consider folding its entire operation.

Somehow, five teams found the funds to play in 1954. One team, the Rockford Peaches, was kept afloat by fan donations. Salaries were reduced, and teams no longer had the money to rent buses. Clubs traveled from town to town in players' cars. Only the Peaches and the South Bend Blue Sox remained from the league's first season of 1943.

Most everyone—league officials, fans, and players— knew the AAGPBL was on its last legs. There was little money and not enough talent on the field. "I could see it coming," said South Bend pitcher-first basewoman Glenna Sue Kidd.[14]

For 12 seasons, the AAGPBL thrilled fans throughout the upper Midwest and beyond. Few people would have believed it possible when Wrigley announced his intention to form a women's professional league in 1943. His dream was realized by the dedication and hard work of more than 600 young women athletes and the devoted fans who supported them.

A SEGREGATED LEAGUE

No black women ever played in the All-American Girls Professional Baseball League—even after Jackie Robinson broke baseball's major league color barrier in 1947. Several Spanish-speaking, light-skinned Cubans were recruited, but African-American women had no opportunity to play baseball professionally in the AAGPBL. Two black women—Elizabeth Jackson and Marie Mazier—tried out with the South Bend Blue Sox in 1951 but neither made the team. A third player worked out with the Blue Sox in 1952, but like the others, she was not invited to join the squad. No other black women are known to have tried out in the AAGPBL's 12 seasons of play.

In November 1951, the team directors met to discuss the issue of including black women in the league. "The consensus of the group seemed to be against the idea of colored players, unless they would show promise of exceptional ability," said the minutes of the meeting. "In the event a club did hire one of them . . . none of the clubs would make her feel unwelcome."[15] The directors' reasoning is uncertain. Perhaps they believed black women did not fit the AAGPBL's image of the "All-American" female ballplayer. Another possibility is that the league was already trying to shatter the gender barrier in baseball. Attempting to challenge the color barrier at the same time may have risked negative publicity and resulted in lower attendance at the games.

At the age of 32, Toni Stone signed with the Indianapolis Clowns of the Negro American League, making her the first woman to play for a major league team. In two seasons, she batted .243 and performed well on second base.

CHAPTER FIVE

JEAN FAUT: RHYMES WITH "OUT"

Jean Faut was widely considered the greatest overhand pitcher in the All-American Girls Professional Baseball League. Unlike many other hurlers, Faut was able to make a successful transition from underhand to overhand delivery. In her eight-year career, she pitched four no-hitters, including two perfect games, and was the only hurler to throw a perfect game after the AAGPBL adopted overhand pitching in 1948.

The Early Years

Faut was born in East Greenville, Pennsylvania, in 1925. As a teenager, Faut

Jean Faut was the most accomplished pitcher in the AAGPBL. She had learned overhand pitching at an early age, unlike many in the league who grew up playing softball.

enjoyed watching the East Greenville Cubs, a men's semipro baseball team. One of the team's players taught her the basics of the game and how to pitch. She became so skilled that she began pitching batting practice for the Cubs and also took the mound in a few of the team's exhibition games. After graduating from high school, she worked in a clothing factory and later at a knitting mill, earning approximately $25 a week.

Faut had not heard about the AAGPBL until a league scout contacted her in 1946 with an invitation to attend spring training tryouts in Pascagoula. She jumped at the opportunity. After somehow convincing her mother to allow her to go, she hopped a train and headed to camp. At tryouts, Faut's skills impressed Meyerhoff's staff, and two weeks later, the 5' 4" (1.6 m), 130-pound (59 kg) right-hander was assigned to the South Bend Blue Sox.

Faut began the 1946 season as the Blue Sox third basewoman. "I had a strong arm," she said, "so third was a natural spot."[1] By midseason, South Bend manager Chet Grant moved Faut to the mound, where she pitched underhand. Eager to play daily, she often played third base when not pitching. Quickly establishing herself as a key member of the Blue Sox, Faut's professional baseball career was about to take flight.

Rising to the Top

Known for her pinpoint control and dazzling assortment of pitches—including a fastball, curve, sinker, and change of pace—Faut soon emerged as one of the league's top hurlers. After going 19–13 in 1947, she began pitching overhand the following year. In September 1948, she hurled her first no-hitter, beating the Racine Belles, 7–0. By this time, Faut was managing a second full-time career:

Faut grew up in a baseball-playing family and developed her renowned pitching precision by throwing stones at telephone poles.

she was married with a baby. "I had to go home [after a game], take care of my family, cook and clean, and all of those things," she said.[2]

Faut was on a roll. In 1949, she posted a superb 24–8 record, including her second career no-hitter: a dazzling 2–0 blanking of the Fort Wayne Daisies in which she walked only one batter. Importantly, Faut had led her team from sixth place in 1948 to a tie for first. Although the Rockford Peaches eliminated South Bend in four straight games in the play-offs, the Blue Sox were on the rise, due largely to Faut's mastery on the mound.

Faut turned in another fine season in 1950, posting a 21–9 mark, while leading the league in ERA (1.12), complete games (29), and innings pitched (290). "I started to mature," said the 25-year-old hurler. "You get better, your control gets better. You work on new pitches."[3] In three seasons, Faut had already established herself as one of the league's dominant overhand pitchers.

The Championship Years

In 1951, Karl Winsch, Faut's husband, became the South Bend manager. To avoid accusations of playing favorites, Winsch cut his wife's number of starts and limited her to fewer innings on the mound. Still, Faut won 15 games while notching a stellar 1.33 ERA, third in the league.

Faut's big moment during the regular season came on July 21, when she pitched a perfect game against the Rockford Peaches. She struck out 11 opposing batters, including five of the last nine she faced. Reporting the game, the *South Bend Tribune* described Faut as "a sturdy gal with a lot of heart, a fast ball that hops, and a curve that breaks off like a country road."[4] Commenting on her dazzling performance, the ever-modest hurler simply remarked, "I had a very good game."[5] By season's end, the Blue Sox made the play-offs and Faut was voted the 1951 AAGPBL Player of the Year.

In the best-of-three first round of the play-offs, South Bend topped the Fort Wayne Daisies two games to one. Faut dominated the

A BASEBALL COUPLE

Faut was the only player in the AAGPBL who was married to her manager. Her husband, Karl Winsch, also came from Faut's hometown, East Greenville, Pennsylvania. Winsch was a promising pitching prospect in the Philadelphia Phillies organization. During spring training with the club in 1946, he suffered a serious, career-ending arm injury. After that, Winsch moved to South Bend to join Faut. The couple married before the 1947 AAGPBL season, and in 1948, Faut gave birth to their first son, Larry. The youngster traveled with the team when he was four years old, wearing a little version of the team uniform. In 1951, Winsch was named manager of the South Bend Blue Sox, a job he held until the league disbanded. Under his guidance, the Blue Sox won their only two championships. The couple divorced in 1968.

opposition, winning both games by a score of 2–1. She pitched heroically in the Game Three clincher, giving up just eight hits in ten innings.

The best-of-five championship series featured South Bend facing the defending AAGPBL champion, the Rockford Peaches. After falling behind two games to none, South Bend manager Winsch sent Faut to the mound to keep his team's play-off hopes alive. She hurled a gem, winning 3–2 while striking out 11 batters. After tying the series with a victory in Game Four, the stage was set for the winner-take-all fifth contest. Faut began the game at third base, but when South Bend starter Lil Faralla tired in the third inning, she took over on the mound. The Blue Sox won the game 10–2 and the championship, with Faut earning credit for the win.

The Blue Sox opened the 1952 season with hopes of winning another title. But there were problems in the clubhouse. Several South Bend players objected to various decisions made by manager Winsch, who was known to have a quick temper. "The girls wouldn't talk to me because I was the manager's wife, and he [Winsch] wouldn't talk to me, so I never knew what was going on in 1952. I just played ball."[7]

Faut was determined not to let the squabbling affect her performance on the field. Instead, she put together her best overall year. On the mound, she went 20–2, while leading the league in winning percentage (.909), ERA (.93), and strikeouts (114). At the plate, she batted a career-high .291 with 32 runs batted in and 15 stolen bases.

South Bend rolled to a 64–45 record to finish second in the league and earn a play-off spot. Just before the play-offs began, however, six players quit the team over the friction in the clubhouse. Hopes to win another title looked bleak.

The opening round of the play-offs pitted South Bend against the Grand Rapids Chicks. In Game One, Faut pitched an impressive three-hitter en route to a 2–1 victory. Starting Game Two at third base, she knocked in two runs as South Bend coasted to an easy 6–1 win, returning the club to the AAGPBL championship series, again facing the tough Rockford Peaches.

As in the 1951 play-offs, Rockford won the first two games against South Bend. Facing elimination, the Blue Sox rebounded to win Games Three and Four, setting up a Game Five showdown with Faut on the mound. She turned in her finest clutch performance, scattering eight hits and slamming two triples in a title-clinching 6–3 victory. It was the most glorious moment in Faut's AAGPBL career. "I am most proud of our team for winning the 1952 championship than anything else, because we won that championship with only twelve girls."[8]

Calling It Quits

Faut returned for her final season in 1953. As dominating as ever, she led the league in wins (17), ERA (1.51), and strikeouts (143). She also batted .275 with a career-high four home runs. Once again, Faut was named AAGPBL Player of the Year. Her peak performance occurred September 3, 1953, when she hurled her second perfect game, a stellar 4–0 win against the Kalamazoo Lassies. The victory was her last win of the season—and the last of her superb professional pitching career.

At the end of the season, Faut decided to hang up her spikes for good. Being married to the manager wasn't worth the clubhouse problems. She came to the ballpark to watch a few Blue Sox games in 1954, but watching her former teammates on the field made her unhappy. "I couldn't take it," she recalled. "I would cry in the stands because I wasn't out on the field."[9] To fulfill her

In 2010, Faut and other AAGPBL players were honored during a game at Comerica Park, home of the Detroit Tigers.

competitive drive, Faut took up bowling. She became so skilled that she turned professional in 1960. Faut appeared on the women's pro tour for nearly 30 years, finally retiring in 1988. In addition, the outstanding all-around athlete was an excellent recreational golfer.

In 2012, Faut was inducted into the National Women's Baseball Hall of Fame in Chevy Chase, Maryland. She is also featured in the AAGPBL permanent exhibit at the National Baseball Hall of Fame in Cooperstown, New York.

CHAPTER SIX

DOTTIE KAMENSHEK: FINE AT FIRST

When World War II broke out, Cincinnati native Dorothy (Dottie) Kamenshek hoped to join the army and become a nurse. Her mother, a single mother who worked hard to support herself and her only child, rejected the idea: no daughter of hers was going to enlist during wartime. Seventeen-year-old Kamenshek—a fine softball player in a local industrial league—had no choice but to give in to her mother's wishes. With military service not an option, Kamenshek wondered what she would do in Ohio while the war played out.

Dottie Kamenshek's superb athletic skill made her the best all-around player in the AAGPBL.

Chance of a Lifetime

One day in 1943, a scout from Wrigley's AAGPBL visited Cincinnati. The talent seeker saw Kamenshek play and invited her to travel to Chicago for tryouts. Mrs. Kamenshek approved the idea only because she was certain her daughter would not be selected to play in the new league.

For a moment, it appeared Kamenshek's mother might be right: on the first day of tryouts, someone stole Kamenshek's baseball glove. Still, playing with a borrowed mitt, the left-hander impressed the scouts and made the cut. She was assigned to the Rockford Peaches. Recalling her days in tryout camp, Kamenshek said, "I felt like it was an opportunity. I just had enthusiasm to make it. I thought, this was my chance."[1]

Nicknamed "Kammie" by her teammates, Kamenshek began the season in center field, a familiar haunt from her industrial league days. Two weeks into the regular season, Rockford manager Ed Stumpf moved her to first base. Playing an infield position wearing the AAGPBL uniform presented her with a huge challenge. "When you stooped to catch a ground ball," she said, "the ball would get caught in your skirt, so eventually they [the league] modified it and allowed us to wear it shorter."[2]

Kamenshek overcame the problem and emerged as the finest fielding first sacker in women's professional baseball. She tirelessly practiced her footwork and stretches at the base so she could catch the infielders' throws as quickly as possible. Former New York Yankee first baseman Wally Pipp called Kamenshek the "fanciest-fielding first baseman I've ever seen, man or woman."[3]

Kammie at the Plate

Kamenshek was an outstanding contact hitter, meaning she did not strike out often, and she usually finished in the top five in batting average each year. Not known as a powerful slugger, she had the uncanny ability to spray the ball to all parts of the field—pulling it to right field or hitting

CHARM SCHOOL, 1943

Once Kamenshek was selected to play in the AAGPBL, she was required to attend the Helena Rubenstein charm school arranged by Wrigley and his staff. Kamenshek recalled her experiences:

I think most of us came from very poor families. . . . The rich were going off to finishing schools, and the poor just didn't learn social skills. . . . I had never eaten out in a restaurant until I went to Chicago, so I knew nothing about which fork to use. . . . I just wasn't educated about these things. Charm school was fun. . . . I think we all took parts of it that we thought were good for us, and eliminated the other. We laughed about it like mad, but I think every one of us picked up things from it.[4]

Kamenshek was the face of the successful Rockford Peaches franchise during her ten years in the league.

to the opposite field. Kamenshek was also adept at laying down a bunt. She earned her reputation as one of the league's best bunters by practicing with manager Bill Allington, who took over as field general in the 1944 season. "He taught me bunting," Kamenshek recalled. "He'd have me out there for hours bunting and dropping the ball down on a handkerchief at third base and first base."[5]

"She (Kamenshek) was the greatest ballplayer in our league. . . . She had what I call the three Hs—head, heart, and hustle—besides all the talent in the world as a ballplayer."[6]

—Pepper Paire Davis, ten-year AAGPBL catcher

Kamenshek is remembered as one of the AAGPBL's greatest hitters and all-around ballplayers. Her lifetime batting average of .292 is the highest of all long-time players in the league. She won two batting titles: in 1946 with a .316 average and in 1947 hitting .306. Kamenshek twice finished second in batting average, hitting .334 in 1950 and a career-high .345 in 1951. She also led the league in most hits with 129 (1946) and most singles: 102 (1945), 120 (1946), and 113 (1948). Amazingly, in 3,736 at bats, Kamenshek struck out only 81 times.

During her ten seasons in the AAGPBL, Kamenshek's exceptional fielding and hitting earned her selection to seven all-star teams. In addition to her personal accomplishments, Kamenshek helped lead Rockford to league championships in 1945, 1948, 1949, and 1950, making the Peaches the

SAYING "NO" TO GOING PRO

Everyone who watched Kamenshek perform on a baseball diamond was awed by her abilities—including professional men's teams. In 1950, the Fort Lauderdale club of the Florida International League tried to purchase her contract from the AAGPBL. The league refused—but it wasn't the only party who said no. Kamenshek herself didn't want to make the move. Not only did she say a woman would be at a physical disadvantage playing with men, but she thought the offer was just a "publicity stunt." Years later, she cited another reason: "They offered me less money than I was making!"[7]

In 1999, *Sports Illustrated* chose Kamenshek as one of the top 100 female athletes of the twentieth century.

most successful franchise in league history. A sports reporter for the *Rockford-Register Republic* (Illinois) observed it was "no exaggeration to say that Kamenshek today is one of the really great woman athletes in the country."[8]

The Later Years

Kamenshek retired after the 1951 season, due largely to a back injury she suffered in 1949 for which she wore a brace while playing. But after missing the 1952 campaign, she returned to the Peaches the following year, playing only in the team's home games. It would be Kamenshek's final year playing in the AAGPBL.

In 1958, she graduated from Marquette University with a degree in physical therapy. She served as a therapist in Michigan and then moved to California, where she became head of the Los Angeles Crippled Children's Services Department. Kamenshek held the position until she retired in 1980. She died in 2010 at age 84 and was inducted into the National Women's Baseball Hall of Fame the same year.

"One thing about our league: it gave a lot of us the courage to go on to professional careers at a time when women didn't do things like that."[9]

—Dorothy "Kammie" Kamenshek

CHAPTER SEVEN
DORIS SAMS: ALL-STAR

Doris "Sammye" Sams was destined to make a name for herself as an outstanding athlete. By 1938, at age 11, the Tennessee-born youngster was already gaining the attention of the press. That year, Sams's sharpshooting brought her a victory in the Southern Appalachian Marbles Tournament, qualifying her to move on to the national tournament in Chicago. She was also the top pitcher for a girls' team in a league run by Knoxville's Recreation Department, a squad that won six state titles. By 1946, the friendly, shy, bespectacled teen was ready for the big time.

Doris Sams was a natural at every sport she tried—football, swimming, diving, badminton, and softball—but her favorite sport was baseball.

Impressing the Scouts

In the spring of 1946, Sams learned two teams from the AAGPBL would soon pass through Knoxville. The teams were on their return trip north from spring training in Pascagoula. Urged by a friend, Sams worked up the courage to ask Racine Belles manager Leo Murphy for a tryout. Sams put on a great show for the scouts and made the league. She was assigned to the Muskegon Lassies, where she played from 1946 to 1950. In 1950, the financially troubled Muskegon squad was sold to Kalamazoo, where Sams ended her career.

Sams was one of the few players in the league who excelled at more than one position. The 5' 9" (1.8 m),

145-pounder (66 kg) switched between center field and the mound, throwing with a natural sidearm motion. In her first year in professional ball, 1946, Sams posted an 8–9 record, while batting .274—respectable numbers against the veterans of AAGPBL. With one year of experience under her belt, Sams was ready to shine. Years later, Sams recalled, "Of course I was homesick, like the other girls, the whole first year. But I thoroughly enjoyed every blame day of playing ball."[2]

The Years of Superstardom

Spring training in 1947 was held in Havana. Sams enjoyed the unique opportunity of playing ball on foreign soil, and she was determined to raise her game to another level in the regular season. That year, Sams notched an 11–4 record, with a league-leading winning percentage of .733 and a stingy ERA of .98. At the plate, she hit .280 with 41 runs batted in. The highlight of Sams's second year came in August, when she hurled a perfect game against the Fort Wayne Daisies, winning 2–0.

With Sams leading the charge, Muskegon finished the season with a 69–43 record, capturing first place. In the best-of-five

"I'd never been anywhere, really, except for Muskegon. Havana was real good. They just couldn't believe women could play ball like that!"[3]

—Doris Sams on spring training in Cuba

first round play-offs, however, the Racine Belles outdueled the Lassies three games to one. Racine's lineup included experienced players such as infielder Kurys and pitching ace Anna May Hutchison. "We just fell apart," said Sams. "Youngsters in the playoffs, I guess."[4]

Still, in only her second year, Sams was named the AAGPBL Player of the Year. Pitching and playing outfield, she was also selected to the all-star team at both positions—the only player to achieve that feat in the league's history.

The AAGPBL introduced overhand pitching in 1948—and although Sams made the smooth transition on the mound to fashion an 18–10 record, she was unable to make the adjustment at the plate. She batted only .257, down 23 points from the previous season. Muskegon

Sams was a skilled pitcher, but she loved playing outfield so she could play in every game.

earned another play-off spot but was eliminated by the Fort Wayne Daisies in the first round.

By this time, Sams's remarkable talents were obvious to everyone who watched her play. The 1948 *Major League Baseball Facts, Figures and Official Rules* noted Sams "is possessed of the cool, calm and self-possessed manner . . .

the true attribute of the great performer—and the stuff of which champions are made."[5]

Sams notched another sensational year in 1949, leading the league in batting (.279) and hits (114). She went 15–10 on the mound with a sparkling 1.58 ERA. She won the Player of the Year award again, becoming the first AAGPBL player to win the honor twice. Pitcher Faut would accomplish the feat in 1951 and 1953.

From 1950 to 1953, Sams batted over .300 each year, enjoying her greatest season in 1952. That year, she reached personal highs with a .314 batting average and a league-leading 12 home runs. The dozen homers set a new league record in that category, breaking the previous mark of ten set by Eleanor Dapkus of the Racine Belles in 1943.

Ending an All-Star Career

Convinced the league would not go on much longer, Sams retired after appearing in 46 games during the last half of the 1953 season. "I was twenty-seven years old," she said, "and the bus rides were killing me."[6] During her eight-year stint with the AAGPBL, Sams was named to

> "We rode an old bus, and we pushed it, half the time—an old beat-up bus. . . . We'd be out there, two or three o'clock in the morning, shoving, trying to get that bus to go on up the road."[7]
>
> —Doris Sams on life on the road

AAGPBL players endured many hours on buses as they traveled throughout the Midwest. After eight years in the league, Sams decided she had had enough.

five all-star teams. Her career batting average of .290 is the league's sixth-highest lifetime mark.

After retiring, Sams took a job as a computer operator for the Knoxville Utility Board, a power line company, where she worked for 25 years. She was inducted into the Tennessee Sports Hall of Fame in 1970 and the Knoxville Sports Hall of Fame in 1982. She is also included as part of the AAGPBL permanent exhibit at the National Baseball Hall of Fame in Cooperstown. Sams died in 2012.

CHAPTER EIGHT
DOTTIE COLLINS: STRIKE!

Growing up in Inglewood, California, Dottie Collins (born Wiltse) had a passion for sports, especially fast-pitch softball. Tutored by her father, Daniel, a local semipro baseball player, Collins blossomed into an outstanding ballplayer. By age 16, in 1939, she had already pitched her teams to two Southern California softball championships. After graduating from high school in 1941, she took a job at the Payne Furnace Company in nearby Beverly Hills, making parts for US warplanes. While there, Collins pitched in an industrial league, capturing several championships for Payne.

Dottie Collins was a gifted pitcher with a number of pitches in her arsenal. In the 1945 season, she pitched 17 shutouts among her 29 wins.

By 1944, her widespread West Coast fame earned her a tryout for the AAGPBL.

Making the Team

Bill Allington, one of Collins's former managers from her teen years, arranged the tryout. Allington was a minor league baseball player and manager. In 1944, he became manager of the Rockford Peaches.

Collins impressed league officials at the tryouts in Peru, Illinois, and was assigned to the Minneapolis Millerettes. The team was one of 1944's expansion clubs, which also included the Milwaukee Chicks. Collins notched an impressive 20–16 record on the mound—the first of four consecutive 20-win seasons. In 1945, the Minneapolis club was relocated to Fort Wayne, playing as the Daisies.

The Glory Years

Collins emerged as the ace of the Fort Wayne pitching staff, winning 29, 22, and 20 games in the 1945 to 1947 campaigns. During those years, she struck out 293, 294, and 244 batters

> "Dad was thrilled to death. Mother cried a lot—she didn't want me to leave home. They came out and saw some games one year. . . . a lot of the parents came either once or twice to see some games."[1]
>
> — Dottie Collins

respectively, earning her the title Strikeout Queen. The 5' 7" (1.7 m), 125-pound (57 kg) righty possessed a dazzling assortment of pitches, including a terrific curveball, which she threw both underhand and overhand.

Collins's finest season was 1945. That year, she pitched two no-hitters within 17 days and set a league record with 17 shutouts. Her most remarkable feat, however, was winning both games of a doubleheader—twice! On August 19, Collins hurled complete game victories over the first-place Rockford Peaches by scores of 5–1 and 1–0. Eight days later, on August 27, Collins repeated the feat, beating the Grand Rapids Chicks, 14–0 and 3–1.

Collins's doubleheader sweep against Rockford was memorable for yet another reason: it was the day she met her future husband, Harvey Collins, a World War II serviceman. Harvey Collins had served most of the war in Honolulu, Hawaii, working as a navy supply clerk. While

Dottie toiled on the mound against Rockford that day, Harvey, an avid baseball fan, sat in the stands watching the action. Intrigued by the attractive and talented pitcher, he arranged to meet her after the games and asked her to play golf the next day. Dottie accepted. She and Collins had a great day on the links, and they continued dating in the months that followed. The couple married in March 1946.

Marriage did not change Collins's status as one of the league's premier pitchers. She returned to the mound, going 22–20 in 1946, 20–14 in 1947, and 13–8 in 1948. While married life failed to affect Collins's baseball career, having a child did. In August 1948, after pitching

Collins was instrumental in organizing reunions for AAGPBL players beginning in the 1980s.

the first game of a doubleheader against the Peoria Redwings, she approached her manager, Dick Bass, in the clubhouse and announced her retirement. Collins was four months pregnant. Her first child, Patty, was born in December.

The Final Years

Collins sat out the 1949 season to raise Patty and manage the family's home in Fort Wayne. She decided to start playing again in 1950 because the couple needed the money. In her final season, Collins posted a 13–8 mark as the Daisies finished second in the league behind the Rockford Peaches with an outstanding 62–43 record. During Collins's tenure with the Daisies, the club made the play-offs in 1947, 1948, and 1950—but never won a championship title.

"We were young, and we were having a good time, and we had money in our pockets. I mean, what more could you ask for? . . . [The league] was the greatest thing that ever happened to us."[2]

— *Dottie Collins*

Collins was a founding member of the AAGPBL Players Association, the group that brought together the league's former players to promote the history of the league. She provided the National Baseball Hall of Fame with memorabilia from the league to include in its permanent collection of the AAGPBL. Collins died in 2008 at age 84.

CHAPTER NINE
OUTSIDE THE WHITE LINES

After the AAGPBL folded in 1954, the players went their separate ways. Some went back to their hometowns, whereas others remained in their team cities, enjoying the friendships they had established. Some moved to new locations to begin life anew. Many players returned to playing softball. Others participated in golf, bowling, hunting, and other sports. Some became coaches. Though the women had experienced a unique, once-in-a-lifetime opportunity to test their skills, as noted by Merrie Fidler, "most of them didn't think of their playing days as anything out of the ordinary at the time."[1] In time, that sentiment would change.

The feminist movement mobilized women to seek equal rights and opportunities in many spheres of life. It served to redefine many traditional gender roles.

The Winds of Change

Beginning in the mid-1960s, the role of women in the
United States underwent significant change once again.
With the growth of the feminist movement, American
women were taking more active roles in business,
government, science, education, sports, and other areas.
Interest in women's accomplishments and contributions
to US and world history gradually emerged. The spotlight
eventually fell on the women of the AAGPBL.

In 1976, graduate student Sharon Roepke, a Michigan
resident, began studying the AAGPBL. Her mission
was to find former players and interview them. Roepke
traveled more than 40,000 miles (64,000 km) throughout
the United States and Canada tracking down the players.
Through her efforts, several of the women began
reconnecting with one other. Roepke became one of the
nation's leading authorities about the league, and in 1984,
she created the first set of AAGPBL baseball cards.

In September 1976, shortly after Roepke began her
investigation, Fidler completed her master's thesis at the
University of Massachusetts. Entitled *The Development and
Decline of the All-American Girls Baseball League,* the work
was a detailed study of the league. Fidler shared her thesis
with Roepke, who used it for her ongoing research on
the AAGPBL.

LIFE AFTER BASEBALL

After retiring, some players married and had families. Others returned to school, and many former players joined the workforce. Their occupations spanned many fields of work.

NAME	YEARS PLAYED	OCCUPATION
Bonnie Baker	1943–1950, 1952	Radio sports news director
Dorothy Doyle	1944–1952	Physical education teacher
Thelma Eisen	1944–1952	Telecommunications
Irene Hickson	1943–1951	Restaurant owner
Marilyn Jenkins	1945–1954	Medical technologist, legal assistant, sales
Mary Rountree	1946–1952	Doctor
Joanne Winter	1943–1948, 1950	Professional golfer

Bringing the Ol' Gang Together Again

In approximately 1978, Kamenshek and Marge Wenzell, ex-AAGPBL players, met with June Peppas, a former first basewoman and pitcher, at Peppas's home in Allegan, Michigan. The three women discussed a reunion of AAGPBL players and set about collecting names and addresses. In January 1981, Peppas sent out the first in a series of newsletters to former players. The one-page letter urged the recipients to work together to plan a reunion.

By the summer of 1981, mini-reunions were taking place. In July, Peppas held one at her home in Allegan. At the end of August, several Blue Sox players got together in South Bend. In September, the Fort Wayne Daisies gathered for a weekend of fun and activities, including an exhibition softball game between former Daisies and other players.

The first large-scale reunion took place at a Chicago hotel on July 8, 1982. Fidler described the joyous, emotional gathering as "a heart-bursting, eye-filling scene to behold—the hotel lobby's atmosphere soaked one's soul with love and joy."[2] Other large reunions were held in Fort Wayne in 1986 and in Arizona in 1988. Reunions were held every two to three years until 2000, when they were scheduled for every year.

Two summers before her death in 2013, former all-star and Racine Belle Sophie Kurys joined with league alumni in Detroit to celebrate their shared accomplishments.

The Doors to the Hall Are Open!

Reconnecting and reliving warm memories with former AAGPBL comrades was rewarding—but the women also wanted to tell their story to world. They wished to have an AAGPBL archives and display at the National Baseball Hall of Fame in Cooperstown.

The road to recognition by the Hall of Fame began in 1984, when Roepke and ex-player Rita Moellering met with Ted Spencer, the Hall's curator. Roepke proposed the idea of an AAGPBL exhibit, but Spencer indicated he wasn't very knowledgeable about the league. She gave him some written information about the league as well as a set of the AAGPBL baseball cards she had recently produced. Spencer was impressed and began considering the idea.

Many months passed, however, with no visible progress being made. In January 1987, an article in the *Los Angeles Times* indicated Spencer confirmed the Hall's plans to create a display about the history of women in baseball, with the focus on the All-American Girls Professional Baseball League. The Hall wanted to consider *all* women who played baseball from the 1800s to the present. The All-Americans, however, wanted a display of their own.

Finally, in April 1988, a compromise was reached. The AAGPBL agreed to be part of a Women in Baseball permanent

"When they played baseball in the AAGPBL, they felt blessed just to be able to play the game they loved at the highest level. They never dreamed of Cooperstown because they were girls (women)."[3]

—Merrie A. Fidler, AAGPBL historian, The Origins and History of the All-American Girls Professional Baseball League

Forty-seven former AAGPBL players met for a reunion at the National Baseball Hall of Fame in 2012.

exhibit. In exchange, the Hall consented to holding a formal unveiling of the display, something it had never done before. In early November 1988, 150 ex-AAGPBL players and their families attended the unveiling ceremony of the Women in Baseball exhibit. A crowd of nearly 1,200 well-wishers was on hand to celebrate the big event. Women in Baseball would become one of the Hall of Fame's most popular exhibits. To this day, ex-AAGPBL players send the Hall memorabilia from their personal collections to update the display.

The AAGPBL on the Silver Screen

One of the attendees at the unveiling of the Women in Baseball exhibit at the Hall of Fame was actress and filmmaker Penny Marshall. Motivated by the courageous women of the AAGPBL, Marshall, an avid baseball fan, decided to make a movie about the players and the league.

Many ex-AAGPBL players helped promote the film, *A League of Their Own*, before it was released in 1992. The women, then in their sixties or seventies, gave interviews on radio and television and to newspapers. By the time the movie opened at theaters in July, news of the league's existence had spread throughout the country.

A League of Their Own was a smash success, increasing awareness of the women players to never-before-imagined heights. "If it hadn't been for that movie, we all would've been dead and gone and no one would have ever known about us," said Peoria Redwings catcher Terry Donahue.[4] According to Fidler, former players became celebrities: inducted into local baseball halls of fame, asked to teach youngsters the basics of the game, and invited to throw out the first pitch at Major League Baseball stadiums throughout the nation. The women of the AAGPBL had played hundreds and hundreds of ball games during hot midwestern summers. But now, at long last, they finally had their day in the sun.

Actor Tom Hanks, portraying the Rockford manager, delivers the iconic line of *A League of Their Own* to actress Bitty Schram: "There's no crying in baseball!"

The players of the AAGPBL were pioneers: they did what no women before them had done. Young and hopeful, they seized the opportunity to do what they loved best—play baseball—and proved to the world that women, if given a chance, could play ball at its highest level.

TIMELINE

1866
The first organized women's baseball teams in the United States start at Vassar College.

1867
A team of African-American women, the Dolly Vardens, is the first professional baseball club in the United States for either men or women.

1890
W. S. Franklin organizes the Young Ladies Baseball Club #1 to play against men's teams across the United States and Canada.

1890s–1930s
Women's Bloomer Girls teams play men's local, semipro, and minor league squads throughout the United States.

1925
The all-female Philadelphia Bobbies travel to Japan to play exhibition games against men's teams.

1941
In December, Japan attacks US naval forces at Pearl Harbor, Hawaii. Tens of thousands of American men and women, including major league baseball players, join the armed forces.

1943
In February, Philip K. Wrigley announces his plans to form the All-American Girls Softball League; in May, the league begins its first season with four teams.

1944
The season begins with a new league name, the All-American Girls Professional Ball League (AAGPBL), and two new teams for a total of six teams; at the end of the season, Wrigley sells the league to Arthur Meyerhoff.

1945
In August, World War II ends; in the third season, AAGPBL attendance soars to 450,000.

1946
In April, spring training is conducted in Pascagoula, Mississippi; in May, the league begins its fourth season with eight teams; the ball size is reduced to 11 inches (28 cm), and sidearm pitching is allowed; attendance climbs to 750,000.

1947
Pitchers are required to throw sidearm; spring training is held in Havana, Cuba.

1948

Overhand pitching is allowed; with new squads formed in Chicago and Springfield (Illinois), the league begins its most successful year with ten teams; more than 910,000 fans see AAGPBL games.

1949

The seventh season begins with eight teams; attendance drops, signaling the beginning of the league's financial woes.

1950

Attendance continues to decline; at the end of the season, team directors purchase the league from Meyerhoff and operate their teams independently.

1951

Team revenues and media coverage drop as more fans pursue a new form of entertainment: television; at season's end, the Kenosha Comets and the Peoria Redwings withdraw from the league.

1952

The AAGPBL begins its tenth season with six teams.

1953

Total debt of the six remaining teams exceeds $80,000, prompting the league to consider shutting down.

1954

Only five teams play in the twelfth and final season of the league, sometimes relying on fan donations to stay afloat; in September, all five teams fold. The AAGPBL ceases operation.

1988

The National Baseball Hall of Fame opens its permanent Women in Baseball exhibit.

1992

In July, the film about the AAGPBL, *A League of Their Own*, debuts at theaters throughout the United States.

ESSENTIAL FACTS

KEY FIGURES

- Philip K. Wrigley, owner of the Chicago Cubs and chewing gum manufacturer, formed what would come to be known as the All-American Girls Professional Baseball League (AAGPBL) in 1943.

- Advertising executive Arthur Meyerhoff helped develop the clean-cut image of the league's ballplayers. He also handled many administrative and financial duties.

- Dorothy Kamenshek was widely considered one of the greatest ballplayers in AAGPBL history.

- Actress-filmmaker Penny Marshall made a movie about the women ballplayers called *A League of Their Own*.

KEY STATISTICS

- In its 12 seasons of play from 1943 to 1954, nearly 600 women competed in the AAGPBL.

- Fourteen different cities in the Midwest hosted a team during the league's existence. Only the Rockford Peaches and the South Bend Blue Sox played all 12 seasons.

- League attendance reached its peak of 910,000 in the 1948 season.

IMPACT ON SOCIETY

The AAGPBL was more than a publicity gimmick cooked up by midwestern businessmen. It was serious baseball, played by talented women athletes who were given the opportunity to showcase their skills on a baseball diamond. The women performed like their major league male counterparts: they slugged home runs, dived for balls, hustled around the bases, and endured long road trips in crowded buses traveling from city to city. Most important, the players of the AAGPBL— together with other American women working in wartime factories and in the armed forces—helped create a new understanding of what women could do. By demonstrating that they were determined, strong, skillful, and athletic, they contributed to women no longer being viewed as the gentler, weaker sex.

QUOTE

"The eight seasons I played in the All-American Baseball League were the most exciting, memorable years of my life. . . . The tougher it got, the more I liked it. The experience gave me self-confidence that I needed to be successful in the jobs I had after baseball."

—Jean Faut, AAGPBL pitcher

GLOSSARY

BATTING AVERAGE

A measure of a batter's performance obtained by dividing the number of base hits by the number of times at bat. Top players in the AAGPBL had an average above .260.

CHAPERONE

A person who accompanies and supervises a young person in public.

CLUBHOUSE

A locker room used by an athletic team.

EARNED RUN AVERAGE (ERA)

A statistic used to measure a pitcher's effectiveness, calculated as nine times the number of earned runs divided by the number of innings pitched. An ERA of 3.0 or under was considered good in the AAGPBL.

FRANCHISE

An authorization granted by a government or company to an individual or group enabling them to carry out specified commercial activities.

INDUCT

To admit as a member.

NO-HITTER

A game in which a pitcher does not allow any hits.

PERFECT GAME

A game in which no opposing batter reaches first base.

PROFESSIONAL
Taking part in an activity for pay, as a full-time occupation.

PROMOTER
An active supporter; a person in charge of publicity and finance.

RATION
To set limits on the amount of certain foods or materials a population can purchase during war or other conflicts.

RECRUIT
To seek new members or employees.

REUNION
A gathering of the members of a group who have been separated.

SEMIPRO
Taking part in an activity for pay, but not as a full-time occupation.

SHUTOUT
A game or contest in which one side fails to score.

UNDERHAND
Performed with the hand kept below shoulder level.

ADDITIONAL
RESOURCES

SELECTED BIBLIOGRAPHY

Browne, Lois. *Girls of Summer: In Their Own League*. Toronto, Canada: Harper, 1992. Print.

Fidler, Merrie A. *The Origins and History of the All-American Girls Professional Baseball League*. Jefferson, NC: McFarland, 2006. Print.

Gregorich, Barbara. *Women at Play: The Story of Women in Baseball*. New York: Harcourt, 1993. Print.

Sargent, Jim. *We Were the All-American Girls: Interviews with Players of the AAGPBL, 1943–1954*. Jefferson, NC: McFarland, 2013. Print.

FURTHER READINGS

Edwards, Sue Bradford. *Women in Sports*. Minneapolis: Abdo, 2016. Print.

Heaphy, Leslie A., and Mel Anthony May (eds.) *Encyclopedia of Women and Baseball*. Jefferson, NC: McFarland, 2006. Print.

Madden, W. C. *The All-American Girls Professional Baseball League Record Book*. Jefferson, NC: McFarland, 2008. Print.

WEBSITES

To learn more about Hidden Heroes, visit **booklinks.abdopublishing.com**. These links are routinely monitored and updated to provide the most current information available.

FOR MORE INFORMATION

For more information on this subject, contact or visit the following organizations:

THE HISTORY MUSEUM
808 West Washington Street
South Bend, IN 46601
574-235-9664
http://historymuseumsb.org/
The museum's AAGPBL collection includes photos, player scrapbooks, rule books, videos of games, scorecards, and programs.

NATIONAL BASEBALL HALL OF FAME AND MUSEUM
25 Main Street
Cooperstown, NY 13326
607-547-7200
http://baseballhall.org/
The museum offers thousands of artifacts, photos, and audio/video recordings that tell the history of baseball from its earliest beginnings.

SOURCE NOTES

CHAPTER 1. PLAY BALL!

1. Lois J. Youngen. "A League of Our Own" in *Baseball and the American Dream: Race, Class, Gender and the National Pastime.* Robert Elias, ed. Armonk, NY: Sharpe, 2001. Print. 253.

2. John Thorn. "Our Game" in *Total Baseball.* Thorn, Palmer, Gershman, and Pietrusza, eds. New York: Viking/Penguin, 1997. Print. 6.

3. Bart Giamatti. *Take Time for Paradise.* New York: Summit, 1989. Print. xx.

4. Robert Elias, ed. *Baseball and the American Dream: Race, Class, Gender and the National Pastime.* Armonk, NY: Sharpe, 2001. Print. 8–9.

5. Barbara Gregorich. *Women at Play: The Story of Women in Baseball.* New York: Harcourt, 1993. Print. 85.

CHAPTER 2. NOT FOR BOYS ONLY

1. Gai Ingham Berlage. *Women in Baseball: The Forgotten History.* Westport, CT: Praeger, 1994. Print. 9.

2. Ibid. 17.

3. Debra Shattuck. "Playing a Man's Game: Women and Baseball in the United States, 1866–1954" in *Baseball History from Outside the Lines.* John E. Dreifort, ed. Lincoln, NE: U of Nebraska P, 2001. Print. 200.

4. *Cincinnati Enquirer.* 6 October 1905. Quoted in Marilyn Cohen. *No Girls in the Clubhouse: The Exclusion of Women from Baseball.* Jefferson, NC: McFarland, 2009. Print. 30.

5. *New York Tribune.* 20 March 1890. Quoted in Marilyn Cohen. *No Girls in the Clubhouse: The Exclusion of Women from Baseball.* Jefferson, NC: McFarland, 2009. Print. 30.

6. Debra Shattuck. "Playing a Man's Game: Women and Baseball in the United States, 1866–1954" in *Baseball History from Outside the Lines.* John E. Dreifort, ed. Lincoln, NE: U of Nebraska P, 2001. Print. 202–203.

7. Berlage, Gai Ingham. "Women, Baseball, and the American Dream" in *Baseball and the American Dream: Race, Class, Gender and the National Pastime.* Robert Elias, ed. Armonk, NY: Sharpe, 2001. Print. 240.

8. Susan E. Johnson. *When Women Played Hardball.* Seattle, WA: Seal, 1994. Print. 140.

CHAPTER 3. THE BIRTH OF THE AAGPBL

1. Linda George and Kenneth Ferraro, eds. *Handbook of Aging and the Social Sciences.* San Diego, CA: Academic Press, 2015. 236. *Google Books.* Web. 2 Aug. 2016.

2. Merrie A. Fidler. *The Origins and History of the All-American Girls Professional Baseball League.* Jefferson, NC: McFarland, 2006. Print. 33.

3. Ibid.

4. Lois Browne. *Girls of Summer: In Their Own League.* Toronto, Canada: HarperCollins, 1992. Print. 25.

5. "League Rules of Conduct." Official Website of the AAGPBL. All-American Girls Professional Baseball League Players Association. 2016. Web. 9 August 2016.

6. Sue Macy. *A Whole New Ball Game: The Story of the All-American Girls Professional Baseball League.* New York: Henry Holt, 1993. Print. 10.

7. "League History." Official Website of the AAGPBL. All-American Girls Professional Baseball League Players Association. 2016. Web. 22 Jul. 2016; Lois Browne. *Girls of Summer: In Their Own League.* Toronto, Canada: HarperCollins, 1992. Print. 24.

8. Carol J. Pierman. "Baseball, Conduct, and True Womanhood." *Women's Studies Quarterly.* 33:1–2, 2005. Print. 68.

9. Lois Browne. *Girls of Summer: In Their Own League.* Toronto, Canada: HarperCollins, 1992. Print. 41.

10. Merrie A. Fidler. *The Origins and History of the All-American Girls Professional Baseball League.* Jefferson, NC: McFarland, 2006. Print. 170.

11. *Kenosha Evening News.* 18 June 1943. Quoted in Merrie A. Fidler. *The Origins and History of the All-American Girls Professional Baseball League.* Jefferson, NC: McFarland, 2006. Print. 60.

12. Ibid.

13. Merrie A. Fidler. *The Origins and History of the All-American Girls Professional Baseball League.* Jefferson, NC: McFarland, 2006. Print. 173.

14. "League History." Official Website of the AAGPBL. All-American Girls Professional Baseball League Players Association. 2016. Web. 6 June 2016.

CHAPTER 4. THE RISE AND DECLINE OF THE AAGPBL

1. Merrie A. Fidler. *The Origins and History of the All-American Girls Professional Baseball League.* Jefferson, NC: McFarland, 2006. Print. 68.

2. Jim Sargent. *We Were the All-American Girls: Interviews with Players of the AAGPBL, 1943–1954.* Jefferson, NC: McFarland, 2013. Print. 11.

3. Lois Browne. *Girls of Summer: In Their Own League.* Toronto, Canada: HarperCollins, 1992. Print.

109.

4. Jim Sargent. *We Were the All-American Girls: Interviews with Players of the AAGPBL, 1943–1954.* Jefferson, NC: McFarland, 2013. Print. 11.

5. Susan E. Johnson. *When Women Played Hardball.* Seattle, WA: Seal, 1994. Print. 23.

6. Lois Browne. *Girls of Summer: In Their Own League.* Toronto, Canada: HarperCollins, 1992. Print. Photo section.

7. Ibid. 135.

SOURCE NOTES
CONTINUED

8. Jim Sargent. *We Were the All-American Girls: Interviews with Players of the AAGPBL, 1943–1954.* Jefferson, NC: McFarland, 2013. Print. 14.

9. Lois Browne. *Girls of Summer: In Their Own League.* Toronto, Canada: HarperCollins, 1992. Print. 181.

10. Merrie A. Fidler. *The Origins and History of the All-American Girls Professional Baseball League.* Jefferson, NC: McFarland, 2006. Print. 137.

11. Ibid.

12. "AAGPBL League Teams by Season." Official Website of the AAGPBL. All-American Girls Professional Baseball League Players Association. 2016. Web. 22 Jul. 2016.

13. Sue Macy. *A Whole New Ball Game: The Story of the All-American Girls Professional Baseball League.* New York: Henry Holt, 1993. Print. 71.

14. Jim Sargent. *We Were the All-American Girls: Interviews with Players of the AAGPBL, 1943–1954.* Jefferson, NC: McFarland, 2013. Print. 22.

15. Merrie A. Fidler. *The Origins and History of the All-American Girls Professional Baseball League.* Jefferson, NC: McFarland, 2006. Print. 190.

CHAPTER 5. JEAN FAUT: RHYMES WITH "OUT"

1. Barbara Gregorich. *Women at Play: The Story of Women in Baseball.* New York: Harcourt, 1993. Print. 143.

2. Jim Sargent. "Faut, Jean." Official Website of the AAGPBL. All-American Girls Professional Baseball League Players Association. 2016. Web. 9 Jun. 2016.

3. Jim Sargent and Robert M. Gordon. *The South Bend Blue Sox: A History of the All-American Girls Professional Baseball League Team and Its Players, 1943-1954.* Jefferson, NC: McFarland & Company, 2012. Print. 145.

4. Ibid. 193.

5. Jim Sargent. "Faut, Jean." Official Website of the AAGPBL. All-American Girls Professional Baseball League Players Association. 2016. Web. 9 Jun. 2016.

6. Jim Sargent. *We Were the All-American Girls: Interviews with Players of the AAGPBL, 1943–1954.* Jefferson, NC: McFarland, 2013. Print. 175.

7. Ibid. 171.

8. Ibid. 170–171.

9. Ibid. 172.

CHAPTER 6. DOTTIE KAMENSHEK: FINE AT FIRST

1. Susan E. Johnson. *When Women Played Hardball.* Seattle, WA: Seal, 1994. Print. 167.

2. Nicole Sweeney Etter. "Fanciest-Fielding First Baseman Ever." *Marquette Magazine.* Marquette University. 2016. Web. 10 June 2016.

3. Ibid.

4. Susan E. Johnson. *When Women Played Hardball.* Seattle, WA: Seal, 1994. Print. 167–168.

5. Merrie A. Fidler. *The Origins and History of the All-American Girls Professional Baseball League.* Jefferson, NC: McFarland, 2006. Print. 222.

6. Dennis McLellan. "Dorothy Kamenshek dies at 84; women's baseball league star." *Los Angeles Times.* May 22, 2010. 2016. Web. 22 Jul. 2016.

7. Merrie A. Fidler. *The Origins and History of the All-American Girls Professional Baseball League.* Jefferson, NC: McFarland, 2006. Print. 224.

8. *Rockford-Register Republic* (Ill.). 21 August 1950. 22. Quoted in Merrie A. Fidler. *The Origins and History of the All-American Girls Professional Baseball League.* Jefferson, NC: McFarland, 2006. Print. 225.

9. Barbara Gregorich. *Women at Play: The Story of Women in Baseball.* New York: Harcourt, 1993. Print. 95.

CHAPTER 7. DORIS SAMS: ALL-STAR

1. Jim Sargent. "Sams, Doris 'Sammye.'" Official Website of the AAGPBL. All-American Girls Professional Baseball League Players Association. 2016. Web. 11 Jun. 2016.

2. Ibid.

3. Jim Sargent. *We Were the All-American Girls: Interviews with Players of the AAGPBL, 1943–1954.* Jefferson, NC: McFarland, 2013. Print. 223.

4. Jim Sargent. "Sams, Doris 'Sammye.'" Official Website of the AAGPBL. All-American Girls Professional Baseball League Players Association. 2016. Web. 11 Jun. 2016.

5. W.G. Nicholson. "*Women's Pro Baseball Packed the Stands . . . Then Johnny Came Marching Home.*" WomenSports. April 1976. Print. 33.

6. Jim Sargent. *We Were the All-American Girls: Interviews with Players of the AAGBPL, 1943–1954.* Jefferson, NC: McFarland, 2013. Print. 227.

7. Ibid. 226.

CHAPTER 8. DOTTIE COLLINS: STRIKE!

1. Jim Sargent. *We Were the All-American Girls: Interviews with Players of the AAGBPL, 1943–1954.* Jefferson, NC: McFarland, 2013. Print. 34.

2. Ibid. 34.

CHAPTER 9. OUTSIDE THE WHITE LINES

1. Merrie A. Fidler. *The Origins and History of the All-American Girls Professional Baseball League.* Jefferson, NC: McFarland, 2006. Print. 229.

2. Ibid. 238.

3. Ibid. 261.

4. Ibid. 286.

INDEX

ABOUT THE
AUTHOR

Nel Yomtov is an award-winning author of nonfiction books and graphic novels for young readers. His writing passions include history, geography, military, nature, sports, biographies, and careers. Yomtov has also written, edited, and colored hundreds of Marvel comic books. Nel has served as editorial director of a children's nonfiction book publisher and as executive editor of Hammond World Atlas book division. Nel lives in the New York City area with his wife.